A DORLING KINDERSLEY BOOK

Editor Lara Tankel
Senior Editor Mary Ling
Designer Helen Melville
US Editor Camela Decaire
Additional Design Sarah Wright-Smith,
Mike Buckley
Managing Editor Sheila Hanly
Production Josie Alabaster
Photography Lynton Gardiner
Illustrator Derek Matthews
Consultant 1st Officer Louise Lipman

First American Edition, 1995
2 4 6 8 10 9 7 5 3 1

Published in the United States by
Dorling Kindersley Publishing, Inc., 95 Madison Avenue
New York, New York 10016

A catalog record is available from the Library of Congress.

ISBN: 0-7894-0211-4

Color reproduction by Chromagraphics, Singapore
Printed and bound in Italy by L.E.G.O.

The publisher would like to thank the following for their
kind permission to reproduce their photographs:
t=top, b=bottom, c=center, l=left, r=right
Robert Harding Picture Library 7t;/Ian Griffiths 5b, 11t; Quadrant
Picture Library/Flight 17c;/McBain 4tl;
Pictures Colour Library 6/7c;
Tony Stone Images 17b/Mark Wagner 17t.

Every effort has been made to trace the copyright holders
and we apologize in advance for any unintentional
omissions. We would be pleased to insert the
appropriate acknowledgment in any subsequent
edition of this publication.

Scale
Look out for drawings like
this – they show the size of
the machines compared
with people.

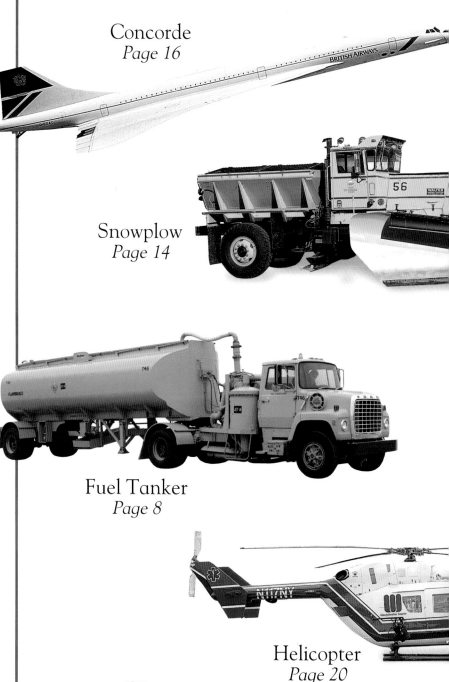

Mighty Machines

AIRPLANE

Christopher Maynard

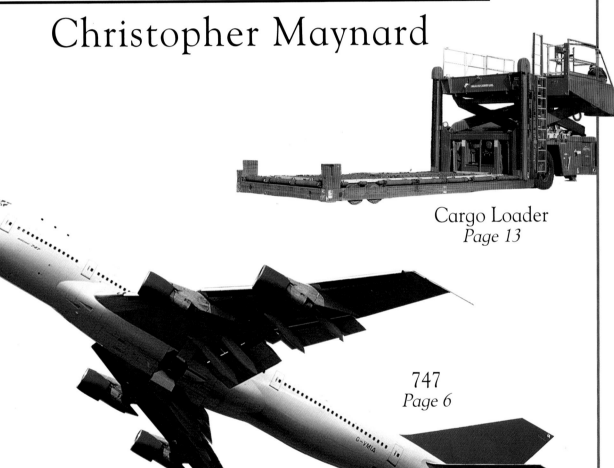

Cargo Loader
Page 13

747
Page 6

The Citation
Page 11

DORLING KINDERSLEY
LONDON • NEW YORK • STUTTGART

747

AMAZING FACTS

Cabin air is so dry that sliced bread turns hard in a few minutes.

The 747 "jumbo jet" is the biggest airliner in the world. The plane has four huge jet engines that propel it along at 580 mph (930 kph). A jumbo jet can carry more than 400 passengers and their luggage for 8,000 miles (13,000 km) before it needs to refuel.

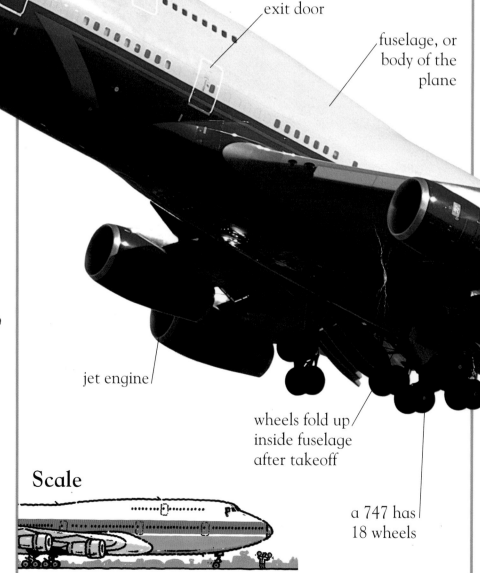

nose wheel

emergency exit door

fuselage, or body of the plane

A jumbo jet is 212 ft (64 m) wide between wingtips – the width of 35 station wagons parked side by side.

Just painting an airline's colors on a 747 can add the weight of a big horse to the plane.

A fully loaded jumbo jet weighs more than 70 elephants.

jet engine

wheels fold up inside fuselage after takeoff

Scale

a 747 has 18 wheels

Hot gases rush out the back of the engines to push a **jet** plane along.

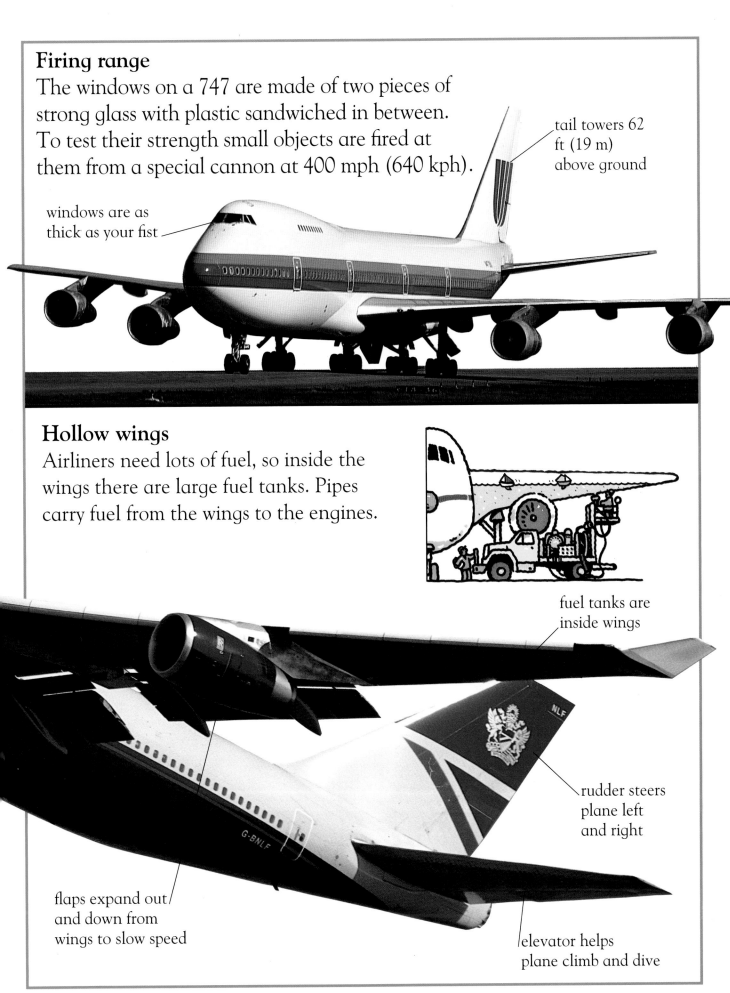

Firing range

The windows on a 747 are made of two pieces of strong glass with plastic sandwiched in between. To test their strength small objects are fired at them from a special cannon at 400 mph (640 kph).

tail towers 62 ft (19 m) above ground

windows are as thick as your fist

Hollow wings

Airliners need lots of fuel, so inside the wings there are large fuel tanks. Pipes carry fuel from the wings to the engines.

fuel tanks are inside wings

rudder steers plane left and right

flaps expand out and down from wings to slow speed

elevator helps plane climb and dive

The **tail** is fixed to the fuselage to stop a plane from swinging from side to side.

Fuel Tanker

AMAZING FACTS

In just one minute, an airport fuel tanker could fill the tanks of 32 station wagons.

It takes 54,000 gallons (204,350 liters) of fuel to fill a 747's tanks. That's enough to fill a big swimming pool.

Airplanes must be filled up with fuel before they can fly, so fuel tankers drive around airports like mobile gas stations. They haul thousands of gallons of fuel, and pump it into waiting planes' wing tanks through thick hoses.

pump can deliver 600 gallons (2,300 liters) every minute

Scale

tanker body full of jet fuel

Hutchinson

T46

T46

1863   JET A

FLAMMABLE

EMERGENCY STOP

  A **pump** forces liquid, such as fuel, from one place to another.

Pump it up

Major airports have large reservoirs full of fuel. Underground pipes carry the fuel near to the planes. Pumper trucks then pump the fuel directly from the pipes into the planes through hoses.

rear platform rises to reach airplane wings

hose

driver's cab can be unhooked from the tank

beacon

driver has a clear view all around

NO SMOKING

JET-A

T46

FORD

FORD 8000

NO SMOKING

BATT OFF
SW ON

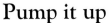 A **reservoir** is a place where liquids are collected and stored for use. 9

Small Planes

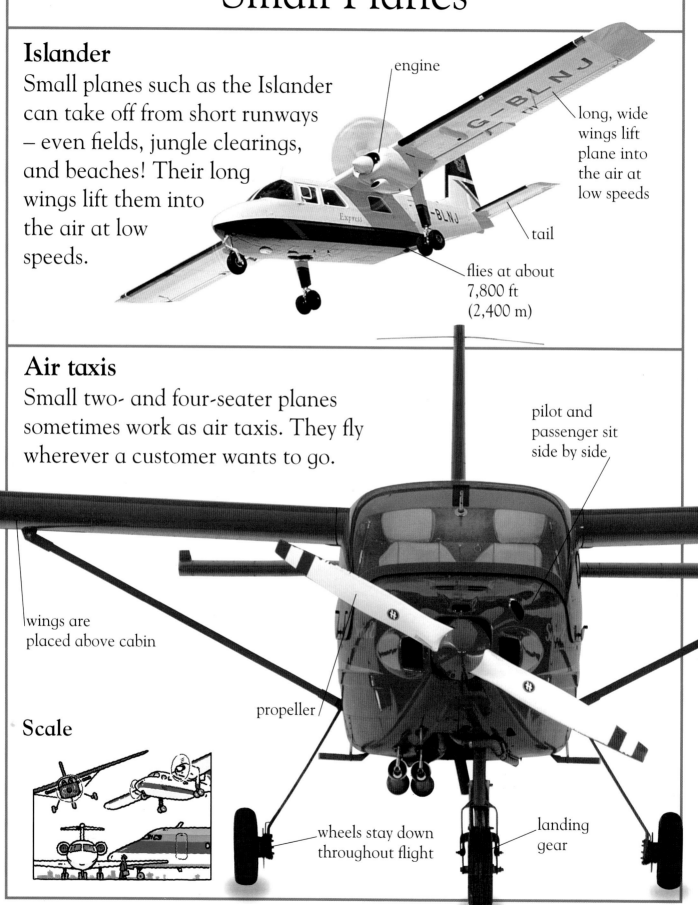

Islander

Small planes such as the Islander can take off from short runways – even fields, jungle clearings, and beaches! Their long wings lift them into the air at low speeds.

engine

long, wide wings lift plane into the air at low speeds

tail

flies at about 7,800 ft (2,400 m)

Air taxis

Small two- and four-seater planes sometimes work as air taxis. They fly wherever a customer wants to go.

pilot and passenger sit side by side

wings are placed above cabin

propeller

Scale

wheels stay down throughout flight

landing gear

The **landing gear** lets an aircraft move safely and smoothly on the ground.

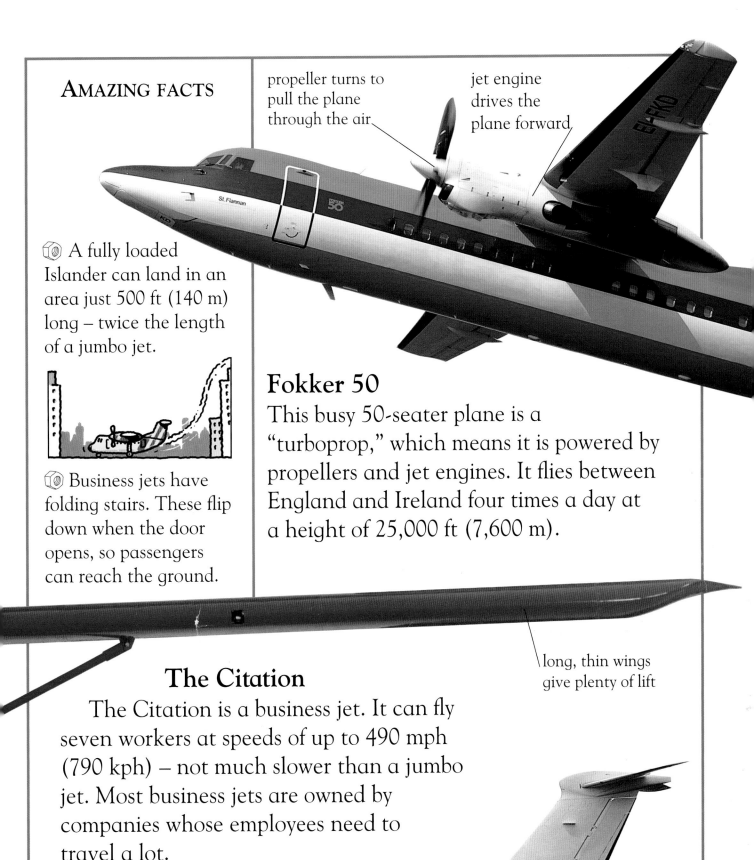

propeller turns to pull the plane through the air

jet engine drives the plane forward

⬡ A fully loaded Islander can land in an area just 500 ft (140 m) long – twice the length of a jumbo jet.

⬡ Business jets have folding stairs. These flip down when the door opens, so passengers can reach the ground.

Fokker 50

This busy 50-seater plane is a "turboprop," which means it is powered by propellers and jet engines. It flies between England and Ireland four times a day at a height of 25,000 ft (7,600 m).

long, thin wings give plenty of lift

The Citation

The Citation is a business jet. It can fly seven workers at speeds of up to 490 mph (790 kph) – not much slower than a jumbo jet. Most business jets are owned by companies whose employees need to travel a lot.

jet engine at the back

🔩 Air flowing over a plane's curved wings creates a force called **lift**. 🔩

Loading Up

Walkways called jet bridges let passengers walk from inside an airport to the door of a plane. They are driven by electric engines and can travel sideways and up and down.

end expands to fit snugly against plane

bridge can move up and down on legs

passengers are protected from weather

wheels can turn in any direction

Scale

Goods carried by an airplane are called the **cargo**. A plane's kitchen is called a **galley**.

AMAZING FACTS

🔩 A big jet with 300 people on board can be unloaded, cleaned, filled with fuel and fresh supplies, and reloaded with passengers and cargo in less than one hour.

🔩 A 747 may have on board 840 meals and 21 gallons (80 liters) of juice – it would take you nearly a year to eat and drink all of that.

Moving meals
Catering trucks, called high loaders, bring carts of food to the door of a plane. They are then rolled into the galley.

loader moves up and down

Baggage ramp
The moving belt of a ramp loader carries luggage up to the cargo hold. It is stacked inside by hand.

Big and strong
A cargo loader handles big, heavy containers. Its rear deck lifts these loads up to the cargo hatch.

tiny wheels move cargo into the hold

🔩 The **hold** of a plane is where the baggage and cargo are stored. 🔩   13

Snowplow

AMAZING FACTS

A snowplow can clear 70 tons (63 tonnes) of snow a minute – enough to make 1,750 small snowmen.

Fully stretched out, a plow's blades are nearly 16 ft (5 m) wide – as wide as five seven-year-olds lying end to end.

A standard runway is 150 ft (46 m) wide – as wide as four tennis courts.

In heavy snowstorms, snowplows are the best machines for keeping an airport open. They carve wide lanes, pushing snow to either side of their blades. Snowplows are followed by snow blowers in a chain of machines that can clear a surface very quickly.

Scale

Blade runner

Six snowplows work together, side by side, to push snow off taxiways. The bottom edges of the plows' blades are made of rubber so they won't damage the surface.

Planes roll along **taxiways** to get from the terminal to the runway.

driver sits
in cab

snow is flung
out of funnel

Snow eaters

Snow blowers chew
through the piles of
snow left by plows and
fling them far to the
side of the taxiways.

snow is drawn
in through
blades

Sweepers

Whatever the
weather, it is very
dangerous for
garbage to get under
a plane's wheels or in
its engines. Small
trucks sweep airport
aprons all day long.

brush
sweeps

large blade cuts
through debris

The **apron** is the area where aircraft park, next to airport terminals.

Concorde

At cruising speed, the Concorde flies one mile in under three seconds – that's faster than a rifle bullet.

The fastest passenger plane is called the Concorde. It flies faster than the speed that sound travels through air, so the Concorde is called a "supersonic" plane.

nose raised for flight

As it shoots along, the Concorde warms up. The tip of its nose becomes hotter than boiling water.

Speed machine
Every part of the Concorde is designed to help it fly quickly. It has wings called delta wings and a thin, sleek fuselage so air passes smoothly over the plane.

slender, cone-shaped nose

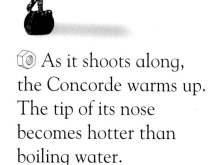

Time warp
The Concorde takes only four hours to fly from London to New York. That's about half the time it takes a 747 to make the same trip.

The Concorde must lower its long nose before takeoff and landing. Otherwise the pilot can't see the runway.

nose dropped for landing

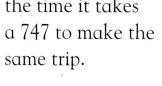

Scale

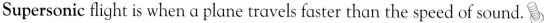

Double glazing
A visor slides up over the Concorde's front windows to make the shape of the nose smoother so air can flow past it more easily.

visor

cabin has room for 100 passengers

cockpit

Travel comfort
The Concorde flies over 49,000 ft (15,000 m) high. There are no gusty air currents at that height to make the ride bumpy, so passengers have a smooth journey.

rudder

Delta wings are special triangular-shaped, swept back wings.

Airport tug

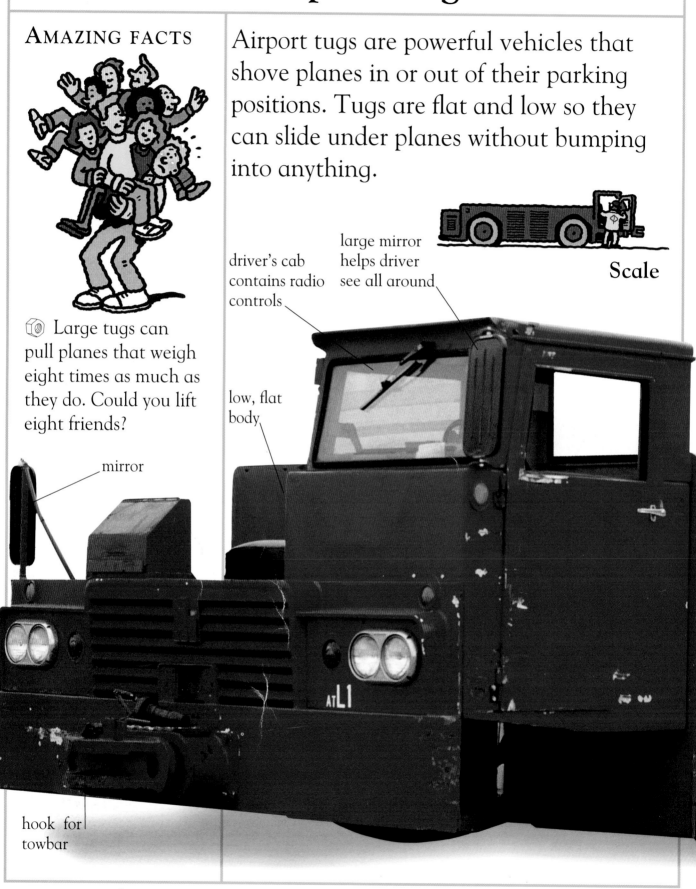

Airport tugs are powerful vehicles that shove planes in or out of their parking positions. Tugs are flat and low so they can slide under planes without bumping into anything.

Scale

Large tugs can pull planes that weigh eight times as much as they do. Could you lift eight friends?

driver's cab contains radio controls

large mirror helps driver see all around

low, flat body

mirror

hook for towbar

The captain and copilot sit in the area called the **cockpit**.

Come in, ground control

A tug driver gets permission over the radio to back a plane from a terminal to a taxiway. He also radios the pilot and copilot, who are sometimes so high up in the cockpit that they can't see the tug.

plane can't move backward on its own

heavy weight keeps the tug from skidding

Mighty shove

A tug hitches a thick steel towbar from its front end to the front wheels of a plane. Then it begins to crawl forward, pushing the plane back.

nearly the whole body of a tug is an engine

extra-wide wheels provide a good grip

 Ground control is in charge of directing all the traffic on the ground at an airport. 19

Helicopter

Helicopters are very different from airplanes. Instead of fixed wings, a helicopter has long, thin blades that spin around and around, pulling the craft straight up into the air. Helicopters can fly forward, sideways, backward, or hover (stay in one place) in the air. This helicopter is an air ambulance.

Scale

rotor whirls the blades around 500 times a minute

blade tip speed is about 450 mph (725 kph)

blades tilt to move a helicopter forward or backward

metal skids

Landing **skids** are used in place of wheels on some helicopters.

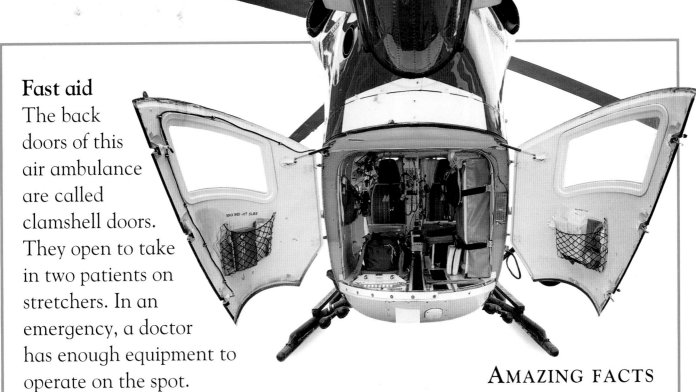

Fast aid

The back doors of this air ambulance are called clamshell doors. They open to take in two patients on stretchers. In an emergency, a doctor has enough equipment to operate on the spot.

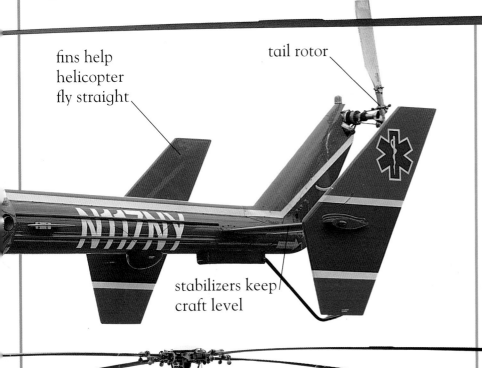

fins help helicopter fly straight

tail rotor

stabilizers keep craft level

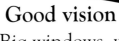

The engine in an average-sized helicopter is about the same size as a backpack.

This helicopter's spot-light shines as brightly as 16,000 candles.

Good vision

Big windows, with windshield wipers just like a car's, allow the pilot to see what is in front and to the side of the helicopter.

 The **tail rotor** stops a helicopter from spinning around under the main rotor. 21